DEDICATION

This book is dedicated to the memory of Colin Clay, flying high now,
who loved children, and taught so many of them how to flap their wings
for the first time.

Learning to Fly
A Shared Journey

Words & Poems by
Adrian Plass

Illustrations & Paintings by
Ben Ecclestone

solway

Solway is an imprint of Paternoster Publishing,
P.O. Box 300, Carlisle, Cumbria CA3 0QS U.K.

British Library Cataloguing in Publication Data

A catalogue record for this book is available from the British Library.

Limited Edition ISBN 1-900507-15-3
ISBN 1-900507-14-5

Printed in Singapore by Tien Wah Press (Pte) Ltd

Contents

INTRODUCTION   9

PLAYGROUND   11

MOTHERS   15

CONFESSING   19

JACQUELINE   23

WILD AFFAIRS   27

LEARNING TO FLY   31

TOO MUCH DYING   35

I CANNOT MAKE YOU LOVE ME   39

UNDISTINGUISHED CORNERS   43

WHAT MAKES YOU CRY?   47

SOWETO 1993   51

THE DOWNS   55

POSTSCRIPT   59

INTRODUCTION

I s it some strange alchemy of shared views and experiences that turns mere acquaintance into friendship? Perhaps, but I think it is a lot more insubstantial than that - more like the way a wine glass can respond to the human voice. Even more like discovering one's ability to sing notes that were previously unattainable, simply by being close to a real singer. My friendship with Adrian has been like that - he being the real singer, of course. I hope I have sung a few worthwhile notes in his direction also.

This book has come out of those received and transmitted resonances. While most of the illustrations and poems have been prepared specially for this project, their origins lie much further back, among shared experiences in the difficult but intriguing business of living.

There is the bitter-sweet remembrance of early expectations and later disappointments. There is wonder at God's creation, and his refusal to abandon us to the consequences of our ill-usage of the world and each other. There is profound enjoyment of simple things, the sounds and sights that are so much a part of personal enjoyment of each day. There is the exhilaration of picking up the things life throws in front of us and making them our own, discovering and exploiting as many possibilities for creative involvement as one can reasonably handle.

There is pain as well, and the frustrated realisation that we have grabbed life by the throat on so few occasions. Many of those who read and look at this book will know exactly what that means.

We have tried to use as much variety in styles of poetry and art as possible, but we certainly do not claim any perfection or completeness for the result. Like its compilers, this book has weaknesses and strengths, and they are all part of our journey. We hope to collect new friends along the way.

Ben Ecclestone

Playground

It seems fashionable to talk about how the previous generation - that graced by Ben and I - was wonderfully happy with much simpler toys and activities than those enjoyed by, for instance, my daughter, Katy, who is eight years old as I write.

"Wasn't it lovely," sigh the nostalgists, "when we used to sit on the back doorstep rolling marbles around in cake-tins and that sort of thing? Why, I can remember," they declaim, almost in tears as enthusiasm hopelessly inflates recollection, "an old dead dog we kids used to play with. Now, to the grown-ups around us it may have been something extremely unpleasant, but, my goodness - to us kids that dead dog would be in turn a pirate ship, or a king's palace, or a proper pump-up football, or a scrummy-yummy feast, or a bugle, or a jet aircraft travelling at twice the speed of sound. We used our imaginations, you see? The whole of one summer holiday that old dead dog kept us happy."

You don't think I'm exaggerating, do you?

Anyway, the point I wanted to make was that we would love the chance to have a go on just a few of the things that Kate's enjoyed in the course of her short life. The soft playground is a prime example. Why should children have all the fun?

Ben and I are putting in applications now for a bouncy castle, to be permanently available on the lawn at the back of our heavenly mansions. In the meantime, we all need to learn how to play, a very necessary attribute for those who really want to fly…

Playground

Oh, God, I'm not anxious to snuff it,
But when the grim reaper reaps me,
I'll try to rely on my vision of Zion,
I know how I want it to be.
As soon as you greet me in Heaven,
And ask what I'd like, I shall say,
'I just want a chance for my spirits to dance,
I want to be able to play'.

Tell the angels to build a soft playground,
Designed and equipped just for me,
With a vertical slide that's abnormally wide,
And oceans of green PVC.
There'll be reinforced netting to climb on,
And rubberised floors that will bend,
And no-one can die, so I needn't be shy,
If I'm tempted to land on a friend.

I'll go mad in the soft, squashy mangle,
And barmy with balls in the swamp,
Coloured and spherical – I'll be hysterical,
I'll have a heavenly romp.
There'll be cushions and punchbags and tyres,
In purple and yellow and red,
And a mushroomy thing that will suddenly sing,
When I kick it or sit on its head.

There'll be fountains of squash and Ribena,
To feed my continual thirst,
And none of that stuff about, 'You've had enough',
Surely heavenly bladders won't burst.
I might be too tall for the entrance,
But Lord, throw the rules in the bin,
If I am too large, tell the angel in charge,
To let me bow down and come in.

We search in vain for grown-ups,
On losing childhood's gem,
And tremble for our children,
When we find that we are them.

Mothers

Ben's mother was ninety-five years old when she died. Grace Ecclestone had a deep, uncomplicated belief in God which easily survived her son's occasional hectoring bursts of theological exposition. Frustrating though these useless debates were at the time, Ben now remembers the simple solidity of his mother's faith with warmth and gratitude. He also remembers that she went out to scrub floors after her husband died in order to raise money for fees when he was a student at the Canterbury College of Art.

Handy with a pudding spoon when Ben was an annoying small boy, and famous for her heavy hints in later life, Grace would have given and done anything for her children because she loved them beyond anyone else, except perhaps that very simple God who received her without theological debate as one of his own in June of nineteen-ninety.

Ben was there when she died. He says it was one of the most peaceful events he's ever witnessed. Her breathing stopped and she slipped quietly from sleep to death.

My own mother is still alive, though confined to a wheelchair, and, in a sense, she becomes more important to me as each day passes. The poem that follows is about her.

Mothers

I remember when my father said
"You'll drive your mother mad if you're not good"
That night I dreamed I had
I saw her sitting on a chair in some sad cell
Nodding, grinning, knowing no-one, driven mad indeed
Lost forever to the wicked child who turned her mind
By being bad
The horror woke me
In the dark my thoughts were white and scraped and raw
I had to call her in to sit beside me looking safely sane
I silently resolved I would be good for ever more
And was – all night.

I remember when I learned at school
Just how the hornbeam leaf can be distinguished from the elm
I told my mother
"With the hornbeam, one side starts a little further down, you see"
She seemed to be so fascinated
Said how she would need to see this for herself
Next day, although a crashing, blowing, soaking storm had broken out
I ran into the woods when school had ended
Searching frenziedly for hornbeam trees and elms
As the weather beat me up I may have cried
But there was so much wet about
I only know I streamed with it and didn't care.

How excited she would be to see it for herself
The way in which the hornbeam is distinguished from the elm
When I got home I'd caught a chill and had to go to bed
But downstairs in the lounge my trophy twigs stood proudly in a vase
And stayed there long beyond the time when they were dead.

I remember all those nights
When I, a pasty teenage renegade
Came creeping home way past the fury hour
No sound, no lights, no comfort for an unrepentant prodigal like me
Except that when I reached out gently in the dark
I'd find a little pile of marmite sandwiches
And touch the chilly smoothness of a glass of milk
My mother put them there because the life of God in her
Gave gifts with all the passion of a punishment
To those she loved beyond reproach
Marmite and milk still comfort me.

And I remember all the pain my mother felt
Through years of staring at a mirror telling vicious lies
About the optimistic child in her
Sad
That so much happiness was spilled and wasted
Drained and lost
Until at last the mirror cracked, and, being on her own
She suddenly remembered who she was
Though God and me – we'd always known.

17

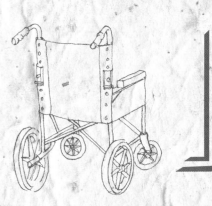

No need for wheelchairs in Heaven.

Confessing

I was inspired to write something about confession after reading an article in an old Christian magazine published in the mid-fifties. The writer was saying how good it was for Mr. and Mrs. Ordinary Christian to have a daily spring-clean of sins committed during the previous twenty-four hours. There's nothing wrong with that, of course. Daily confession has been part of normal Christian living for two thousand years. No, it was the 'Confession Check-list' at the end of the piece that bothered me. This catalogue of the sins that one was likely to commit on a daily basis made for extremely dismal reading. I worked my way miserably through it.

Had I envied someone? Yes I had.

Had I judged someone? Yes, yes, I had.

Had I lusted? Well, yes.

Had I cheated anyone, even in a small way? Yes, probably.

Had I been ungrateful to God? Yes, I expect so.

Had I been untruthful, even in a small way? Yes! yes! yes!

Had I neglected to pray? Oh, shut up!

I think the only thing on the list that I hadn't done was something involving a word that I didn't know the meaning of, and I'd probably have had to confess to that as well if I'd known what it was. Guilty on twenty-nine counts and possibly all thirty! What an encouraging way to start the day.

The writer of the article was only trying to help, but his list was actually in danger of hanging a debilitating necklace of thirty small but heavy lead weights around the necks of his readers. Most of us know only too well that we fail continually, but the way of a penitent child with his father is not to complete a comprehensive check-list, but to throw himself and his failings on the mercy of the Father whom he trusts.

Confession is essential, but it happens within the context of relationship, and it's supposed to result in joy.

Confessing

My conscience is clear about Ghandi's career,
I didn't impede him one jot,
I've never set lions on free-church Hawaiians
(I've wanted to do so a lot).
Nor am I the type to knock out my pipe,
On a twenty-stone Sumo for fun,
And despite all that mess in the Daily Express,
I've never played draughts on a nun.
I fight all temptations to napalm small nations,
It's just as old-fashioned a scheme,
As feeding your panda with maps of Uganda,
However astute that may seem.
I've never bombed Yale nor harpooned a whale,
Nor flirted with visiting popes,
I fiercely resist being lustfully kissed,
By the stars of American soaps.

I'm well in accord with the words of Our Lord,
Where he teaches us how we should pray,
He tells us prayer strength isn't measured
   by length,
So I pray for three seconds each day.
I know God won't bless any tithing unless,
We can cheerfully give, and not fret,
As I don't find it funny to part with my money,
I've not given anything yet.
I ought to feel great in my virtuous state,
Uniquely, a moral success,
So why do I sense there is something immense,
That I urgently need to confess?

21

Wild affairs

Should I have had more wild affairs
In old cathedral towns
Before I got redeemed by God
And had to settle down?

Should I have touched more shining hair
And kissed more pretty eyes
Told through the soft and silky nights
More soft and silky lies?

Should I have crossed the muffled close
And known as evening fell
Through orange light on virgin snow
That all things could be well?

Should I have spent more glowing hours
Behind the leaded panes
Among the overcoats and scarves
The innocent refrains?

Should I have seen with calmer eyes
How tragedies begin
The darkness wrapped in cellophane
The warmth of joy and sin?

Should I have lingered in the streets
To say more morning prayers
As all the world went greyly past
Should I have echoed theirs?

Should I have learned to love the world
Before I let it go
The shadowed marks of many feet
Criss-crossing in the snow?

Should I have taken time to hear
More distant church bells ring
And marvelled at the kingdom
Long before I met the king?

"That which you have never had,
You never want or miss,"
Especially when referring to,
The twit who first said this.

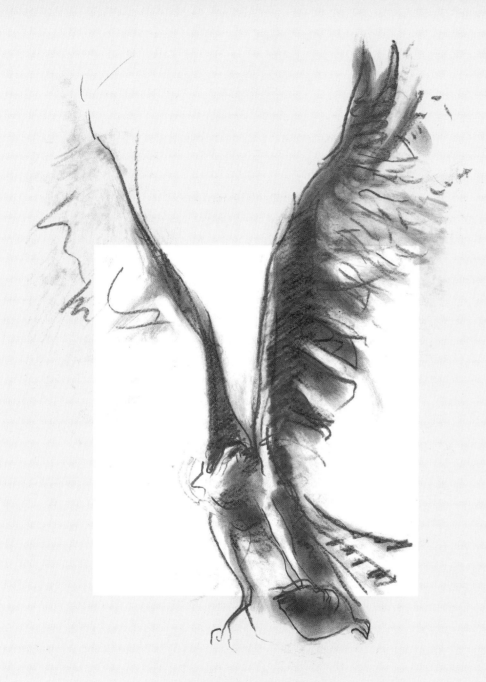

Learning to fly

I seem to recall reading that dreams about flying are supposed to indicate sexual frustration in the dreamer, but I would venture to suggest that there is a much deeper and more fundamental frustration bound up in the yearning to be physically weightless and free (especially if you weigh as much as I do). Do you sense, as I do, that there is a potentially ideal state for human beings, a way of being which can be experienced only at odd moments in this life? Great sporting achievements, the music of Mozart, being in love on a fine spring morning, and whatever you would add to the list – these things can all offer a glimpse of the way we just know things ought to be.

If you asked Ben to make such a list, I know that dancing would be very near the top, not because he's done much of it himself (his wife will testify to that), but because he loves to paint the human body in movement. The intense discipline of dance training produces a freedom and physical escape that, to the observer, looks very much like the beginnings of flight.

Learning to fly

We have stretched our arms towards him,
We have longed to draw him down,
Sought to raise him from the frozen heart of stone,
We have searched the rocky passes with our sisters and
    our brothers,
We have raced through shadowed valleys of our own.
And our fingertips have touched him,
Yes, our fingertips have touched him,
Though we move before his touch can slow us down,
How we grieve that in our turning,
The eternal moment passes,
As our newly floating hopes begin to drown.
And we long for when we rise with him,
Beyond this place of searching,
Moving effortlessly through the new-made sky,
Where the blue could not be deeper,
And a child's sun is smiling,
On the citizens of Heaven as they fly.
Then the rising will not lift us, nor the falling
    bring us down,
And the springs will ring with echoing delight,
But until we spread our wings in the company of angels,
Dancing is the nearest thing to flight.

Too much dying

Too much dying, don't you think?

Too much screeching metal
Sudden impact
Unexpected endings
Too much mindless murder
Too many killer-dogs
Too many children suffocating in abandoned freezers
Too many sad, sad rooms
Too many tears
Too many broken hearts
Too much turning finally away
Too much agony of body, mind, memory
Too much grief melting lives like wax at gravesides
Too many guns
Too much wild, wild callousness
Too little imagination.

We can do something, can't we?
We can support political change
We can prohibit the sale of arms
We can send peace-keeping forces
We can deal with social conditions that cause crime
We can put muzzles on dogs
We can put out more publicity about freezers
We can make it harder to pass the driving test
We can find new ways to slow people down
We can teach kids to be as scared of roads as they are
    of strangers.
We can get something going on Breakfast Television
We can do something, can't we?
Yes, but let's not tell people about Jesus
Let's not make it clear that he hates final endings
    more than we do

Let's not pass on the fact that he has overcome this
    death we dread
Let's not push it down anyone's throat
Even if it's an air way
Let's not offend anyone by mentioning the cross
Or the scream that ripped itself from him when
    the thing was finished
Let's not pass on the news that he came back from
    the dead and lived
Oh, don't tell them that they can do the same
Don't let anyone understand that this tiny corner
    of eternity will pass
Let's not use words like salvation
Redemption
Heaven
Hell
Fire and brimstone are just symbols – aren't they?
Only fanatics would want folk to avoid whatever
    Jesus died to save us from
Let's assure everybody that all religions are beams
    of light
Shining from different facets of the same crystal
For goodness' sake let's keep both feet on the
    ground
Let's be accommodating
Let's be focused
But liberal
Let's compromise
Let's keep the peace
Let's hope, for all our sakes, that when the final
    reckoning is made
We got it right

Too much dying, don't you think?

I think I fear oblivion
more than hell.
Not having to face
either will be sheer
heaven.

I cannot make you love me

A couple of years ago I took a six month break from public speaking of all kinds. The idea was to present my mind to God as a sort of blank sheet of paper. His task, as I envisaged it, was to cover this sheet with a multitude of fascinating spiritual insights that I would then pass on (with suitable humility) to the waiting masses. Forty or fifty of these major revelations would have been quite sufficient, I reckoned – about six in each month.

A rather important flaw in this otherwise faultless scenario was the fact that God was less impressed by it than I was (someone once said that it's easy to make God laugh – you just tell him your plans). After half a year my total score of new insights was precisely 'one' – a poor crop from six months of cultivation.

Having said that, this single scrap of understanding turned out to be a very significant one.

God can be hurt.

That was all it was, and, to be honest, it was more of a logical conclusion than a spiritual one. How can you love someone, I asked myself, without being vulnerable to rejection or attack by the object of your passion? If this is not the case with God's care for men and women, then his feelings for us are so far away from love, as we understand it, that the term becomes meaningless.

God can indeed be hurt, and a primary cause of such hurt is our failure to respond when he reaches out to us. The grief of God rolls across the face of creation like a deep, sad sea. Omnipotent, omniscient and omnipresent he may be, but he will never force anyone to love him.

Understanding this deceptively simple fact might increase our buoyancy just a tad.

I cannot make you love me

If I wanted I could take the light
One shining sheet of paper
Crush it in my fist
And then – it would be night
If I was so inclined
I could destroy the day with fire
Warm my hands at all your charred
    tomorrows
With the smallest movement of my arm
One flicker of my will
Sweep you and all your darkness from the
    land
But I cannot make you love me
Cannot make you love me
Cannot make you love me
I cannot make you, will not make you,
    cannot make you love me

If I wanted I could lift the sea
As if it were a turquoise tablecloth
Uncover lost forgotten things
Unwritten history
It would be easy to revive the bones
Of men who never thought to see their homes
    again
I have revived one shipwrecked man in such a way
The story of that rescuing, that coming home
Might prove I care for you
But though I can inscribe I LOVE YOU in the
    sky and on the sea
I cannot make you love me
Cannot make you love me
Cannot make you love me
I cannot make you, will not make you, cannot
    make you love me

I can be Father, Brother, Shepherd, Friend
The Rock, the Door, the Light, Creator, Son of Man
Emmanuel, Redeemer, Spirit, First and Last, the
    Lion or the Lamb
I can be Master, Lord, the Way, the Truth, the Wine
Bread or Bridegroom, Son of God, I am, Jehovah
Saviour, Judge, the Cornerstone, the Vine
I can be King of Kings, Deliverer, the Morning Star
Alpha and Omega, Jesus, Rabbi, Carpenter or
    Morning Dew
Servant, Teacher, Sacrifice, the Rose of Sharon
I can be – I have been – crucified for you
But I cannot make you love me
Cannot make you love me
Cannot make you love me
I cannot make you, will not make you, cannot make
    you love me

Soweto 1993

South Africa was lovely from the air
But as we spiralled to Johannesburg
We wondered why they'd let those fields of litter
Desecrate the landscape for so many miles around the city edge
Perhaps they didn't care
Perhaps they found it easier to blank it out
Than bother to recycle it or bury it beneath the ground
But is there not a likelihood, we thought
That in the end the problem will grow mountainous
The stench of foul neglect become obscene
Until that mountain falls towards the city
Toppling irreversibly
And covering the part of town that prides itself on staying clean?

When he was forty years old Moses killed an Egyptian and buried his body in the sand. After a further forty years in exile God brought him back to Egypt, not to kill more Egyptians, but to lead his entire nation to freedom.

Given that this is a rather rare task, to say the least, and that Moses must occasionally have longed to swap notes with someone who had been involved in something similar, perhaps we might reasonably conjecture that, in a little corner of heaven, God, in his mercy and wisdom, has provided a small but very pleasant bungaloid mansion with a sign over the door that simply reads:

MOSES AND MANDELA

The Downs

If I travel south from Hailsham for a few miles, and Ben travels north from Hampden Park for a few miles (although he'll laugh when he reads this because he almost always picks me up from home) we are quite likely to meet at the bottom of a very steep hill in a village called Willingdon. At the top of this very steep hill is a place called Butt's Brow, and from there it's possible to walk across our local chalk hills, the South Downs, for about as long and as far as anyone would want to. You can fill your lungs with Heaven up there.

We usually make for a charming little village called Jevington, sitting in a fold in the hills, and featuring, not only a most attractive parish church, but also a public house which it would be a sin to avoid. On those occasions when my wife has kindly agreed to collect our bodies later in the afternoon, we might, having avoided sin, walk over the next hill to a slightly larger and even more charming village called Alfriston, where further temptation in the form of eschewing cream teas and the like must be firmly resisted.

I know of few more enjoyable activities than these walks of ours, all too rare as they are. The idea for this book was born in the course of one of them, and grew up in the course of several more.

I love the Downs. When you're up there you feel it might actually be possible to fly.

The Downs

Why do I love the Downs?
Because they scrunch and rattle
Beneath us as we walk
Brittle bones of flint
Yielding flesh of chalk
Because the sun's unpanicked here, and free
Dawdles on a hilltop
Skips around a bit
Paints a dream of heaven
Gossips kindly with a stunted tree.

Why do I love the Downs?
Because they prove
That valleys can't climb hills
That spirit sometimes rests
When body wills
They've never let us down, the Downs
They raise our kites
Raise our children
Higher, better than we ever could
Down here in temporary, television towns.

Friendship, like cricket
Is a sideways game
From Butt's Brow to Jevington
Hearts are all ears
Eyes study the horizon.

Bridleway to Jevington.

Postscript

There may be some who bought LEARNING TO FLY thinking that it was a small aircraft manual or a chinese cookery book. Such people will be deeply disappointed, and we sympathise.

The others, those of you who have willingly joined Ben and me on our journey through the things that matter to us, are the people for whom we planned and executed these pictures and poems. We hope that, as well as enjoying the things we've produced, you might feel inspired to express your own journey, using whatever talents God has given to you.

Learning to fly is not usually an easy process, but it is the only really worthwhile thing to do, and we have it on good authority that no-one is excluded from making the attempt. God bless you as you spread your wings.